IGNITE

A 30-Day Guide to Get You to Your Next Level and Achieving Your Goals

Devonia Reed

Ignite: A 30-Day Guide to Get You to Your Next Level and Achieving Your Goals

ISBN 10: 0578409690

ISBN 13: 978-0578409696

The Reeding Room

Devonia Reed

www.devoniareed.com

Are you ready to maximize your life and live the life of your dreams? Are you ready to move from surviving to really enjoying life? This guide is designed to get you from where you are, and on the path to where you want to be. It is broken up into three parts:

- Day 1-10   Setting Goals and Developing a Plan
- Day 11-15 Life Applications
- Day 16-30 Accountability

Days 1-15 are designed to get you started, provide practical application, and to keep you motivated. Days 16-30 are accountability pages that you will use to hold yourself accountable to completing what you start.

Complete each "assignment" as it will be essential in helping you to meet your desired goal(s).

I look forward to hearing about how you have grown throughout this journey, and the amazing ideas that are birthed through this process.

Here's to your greatness!

Devonia

Setting Goals and Developing a Plan

Day 1

Identify Your Goal

Decide on a goal you want to accomplish, and what you will gain from achieving this goal. As you complete your 30 day journey, focus on this goal. Completing this sheet will help to reinforce the importance of reaching your goal.

My goal is to...

_____
_____
_____
_____
_____
_____
_____
_____
_____
_____
_____

Accomplishing this goal will...

_____

_____

_____

_____

_____

_____

_____

_____

_____

This is important because...

_____

_____

_____

_____

_____

_____

Day 1

My Daily Reflection

At the end of the 30 days I will be able to...

_____

_____

_____

_____

_____

_____

_____

_____

_____

_____

_____

_____

_____

Day 2

Getting Started

Many times the most difficult thing about accomplishing a goal is getting started. We have ideas that we want to implement, but they remain ideas. Use the worksheet on the following page to make a strategic plan on how you will implement your goal. Identify specific days and times when you will be intentional about the time you will invest in working on your project. Hold yourself accountable by reflecting on your progress or lack thereof.

Day 2

Getting Started

Use this sheet to devise a daily plan for how you will manage your time to achieve your goal. Try to choose the same day and time, consistency helps in developing a habit.

I plan to work to commit to working on my goal:

Monday at (time) _____ for (how long) _____.

Tuesday at (time) _____ for (how long) _____.

Wednesday at (time) _____ for (how long) _____.

Thursday at (time) _____ for (how long) _____.

Friday at (time) _____ for (how long) _____.

Saturday (time) _____ for (how long) _____.

I will commit a total of _____ hours a week working on my goal.

If I miss a scheduled time, I will:

_____

_____

_____

_____

_____

_____

_____

Day 2

My Daily Reflection

I will ensure that I am able to follow my schedule by...

_____

_____

_____

_____

_____

_____

_____

_____

_____

_____

_____

_____

_____

Day 3

Eliminate the Non-Essentials

Use this worksheet to list some habits and/or activities that you can eliminate from your daily routine, and may inhibit you from completing your goal.

Habit #1

_____
_____
_____
_____

Habit #2

_____
_____
_____
_____

Habit #3

_____
_____
_____
_____

Day 3

My Daily Reflection

What habits will be most difficult to eliminate?

_____

_____

_____

_____

_____

_____

_____

_____

_____

_____

_____

_____

_____

_____

Day 4

Consult the Experts

When seeking answers to questions on the best course of action, seek the experts. There are experts in every field of work. Don't try to reinvent the wheel. Learn from people who have done what you are attempting to do, attend workshops that will teach you what you want to know, or get a mentor in your field who can help you to grow professionally. Register for a course where you can learn more about your topic. When finances are a problem, do some research, buy a book written by a leader in your field, or surf the web.

Day 4

Consult the Experts

Document the experts you consulted in your field. What were the results of the "consultation?" Did you make a decision? Did you buy a book? Were you able to take action on something? For example: You did a Google search on where to buy material for an item you want to make. The action you took was to go to the store to buy the fabric.

Expert	Results/Action Taken

Day 4

My Daily Reflection...

How can consulting an expert help you to reach your goal?

_____

_____

_____

_____

_____

_____

_____

_____

_____

_____

_____

_____

_____

_____

Day 5

Be Intentional

Being intentional means that something is done on purpose and is deliberate. It has been planned and decided on well before it happens. Many things we want to get done, don't happen because we are not purposeful. We hope, wish, and pray, but we never actually plan it out or put any action behind what we say we want. Scheduling time to work on your project is a sure fire way to ensure that it gets done. Don't try to fit the project into your busy schedule. Be intentional and schedule specific days and/or times when you will commit to strictly working on your project.

Day 5

My Daily Reflection

What does being intentional mean to you?

_____

_____

_____

_____

_____

_____

_____

_____

_____

_____

_____

_____

_____

Day 6

Check References

Many of us are not a jack of all trades and will likely need to hire others to help us complete and/or work on our project. There is nothing wrong with that, in fact, it's smart to get help from people who have expertise in an area where you may not. It's important however to do your homework when employing the help of others. When hiring people to work on your project always ask for references. If they can't provide references, then you may want to reconsider working with them. When following up with references be sure to ask important questions such as, "How well did the person meet deadlines?" "How well did they communicate?" "Were you satisfied with their work?" "Did they have a good work ethic?" Checking references can save you a lot of time and stress down the road.

Day 6

My Daily Reflection...

Do you generally take people's word for what they can do?

How has that impacted your life?

_____

_____

_____

_____

_____

_____

_____

_____

_____

_____

_____

_____

_____

Day 7

Expand your circle

Expanding your circle can be critical when taking on a new venture. Getting around like-minded people or people who are where you want to be helps with personal growth. It also helps you to get to your desired destination much sooner than trying to achieve it on your own. It helps to be around people who have the same drive that you do, on the difficult days, they can be the push that you need to keep you going. A friend of mine once said," Show me your friends, and I'll show you your future." The people we associate with have a great influence on who we are, but not only that, they impact what we do. If they don't find the things that you are doing worthwhile, they will discourage you to not do it, and won't respect the time you need to invest in it. It would be great if we could take everyone on the ride, but not everyone should go. You have to decide if what you want is worth cutting some ties. Don't be hindered by relationships that no longer serve a purpose in your life. Let go, and surround yourself with people who can motivate, inspire, and encourage you. Find a Meetup group that interests you and join it or start to attend events held by people who you may want to meet. Expand your circle.

Day 7

My Daily Reflection

What relationships to do you need to end?

What can you do to meet new people?

_____

_____

_____

_____

_____

_____

_____

_____

_____

_____

_____

_____

_____

Day 8

Celebrate Milestones

Avoid getting discouraged if the project isn't completed as fast you would like. Progress is key, celebrate the baby steps because they matter. Pat yourself on the back when you meet a deadline or you have figured out how to solve a problem. Celebrate the small wins because you will need them on the days when things are not going as planned. Remember, "The race is not given to the swift or the strong but to he who endures until the end."

Day 8

What can you do to celebrate your small wins?

_____

_____

_____

_____

_____

_____

_____

_____

_____

_____

_____

_____

_____

Day 9

Learn from Your Mistakes

Avoid making the same mistakes again and again. If it didn't work the first time, chances are it isn't going to work the next time. Try a different approach or method that you haven't tried before. Insanity is doing the same thing and expecting a different result. Don't waste valuable time trying to make something work. We can be guilty of this in relationships, but it can be costly in business. If someone hasn't kept up their end of an agreement, do not give them the opportunity to waste your time and/or money again. There are plenty of other options out there, however, it will require that you do your due diligence in finding another way. Time is valuable and it isn't wise to spend it on methods that have proven to be ineffective.

Day 9

My Daily Reflection

How do you bounce back from making mistakes?

_____

_____

_____

_____

_____

_____

_____

_____

_____

_____

_____

_____

_____

Day 10

Do Everything in Excellence

Providing a service or good means nothing if it isn't quality. You want people to continue to seek you out, and they will do that if they are happy with what they received previously. When your name is brought up, you want people to give you a glowing recommendation. Be of good character and trustworthy. The late Myles Munroe said, "Solid character will reflect itself in consistent behavior, while poor character will seek to hide behind deceptive words and actions." If you are unable to provide a service, be honest, it's perfectly acceptable to turn people away if you are unable to fulfill a request. Many times people take on more than they can handle because they want the business, and in return they sacrifice a long term relationship that could have been established with a client/customer.

Day 10

My Daily Reflection

What does excellence mean to you?

_____

_____

_____

_____

_____

_____

_____

_____

_____

_____

_____

_____

_____

_____

_____

Life
Applications

Day 11

Change Your Mind

Les Brown has been quoted as saying. "Change your thinking. Change your life! Your thoughts create your reality. Practice positive thinking. Act the way you want to be, and soon you will be the way you act." Before you can make any changes in your life, you have to change the way you think.

The first step in changing your thinking is to start to be grateful for what you have. Move from viewing problems as obstacles to thinking about them as opportunities. How we think about obstacles or challenges significantly impacts our mood. How many times have you heard someone blame someone else for his/her mood? He made me mad or she made me mad. Often people say, I couldn't help it. Truthfully, we can help it. We can CHOOSE not to get angry, we can CHOOSE not to engage. We can CHOOSE to let it go. It all begins with changing how we think.

Day 11

Change your Mind

Things OUTSIDE My Control

Other People's Actions   Other People's Words

Other People's Mistakes   Other People's Feelings

Things I CAN Control

*My Words   *My Actions
*My Ideas   *My "Play"

*My Effort   *My Mistakes
*My Behavior *My Time

Other People's Ideas   Other People's Behavior

Other People's Time

Reflect on the following questions. Write your responses in a journal, so that you can look back on the later.

- Are my problems a result of the actions of others or my own?

- Do I allow the words and or actions of others affect my mood?

Day 12

Get Out of Your Comfort Zone

Myles Munroe has been quoted as saying, "The graveyard is the richest place on earth because there you will see the books that were never published, ideas that were not harnessed, songs that were sung, and drama pieces that were never acted."

I have found that one of the things that hinders us most from progressing in life or stepping out and doing the thing that we dream about, is the fact that everything is "fine." Many people will never leave jobs that they don't like because they are comfortable. The problem with comfort is, there is no growth. Many of us will never reach our potential because we are busy living a comfortable life. It's time to get uncomfortable.

Day 12

Get Out of Your Comfort Zone

Decision Making Sheet

What decision needs to be made?

_____

_____

_____

_____

_____

_____

_____

_____

Best Case Scenario	Worst Case Scenario

Decision:

_____

_____

_____

_____

_____

_____

_____

Next Steps:

_____

_____

_____

_____

_____

Day 13

Have Faith

Faith is all about believing. You don't know how it will happen but you know it will. The problem that most people have with faith is that it isn't tangible, we can't see it, we can't touch it, but it's one of THE MOST important factors for anyone who wants to change their life. Faith is knowing that it will happen even when, or I should say especially when no one else believes it. One of the most important things a person can possess is faith. "Faith is being sure of what you hope for, and certain of what you do not see."

Day 13

Have Faith

What are some positive affirmations or Bible verses you can recite daily to motivate yourself?

Positive Affirmation

_____

_____

_____

Bible Verse

_____

_____

_____

Positive Affirmation

_____

_____

_____

Bible Verse

_____

_____

_____

Positive Affirmation

_____

_____

_____

Bible Verse

_____

_____

_____

Day 14

Invest in Yourself

Invest in taking care of yourself mentally - Spend time with you. Take yourself out to lunch, get a massage, or get a pedicure. Taking time for yourself is not selfish, it's necessary. We can't keep pouring into other people without first taking care of ourselves.

Invest in your personal growth - Read a book in your area of expertise. Attend conferences and/or seminars on topics where you could use more growth.

Invest financially - Don't let what you see in your bank account prevent you from doing what you know you've been called to do. When we think in terms of lack, we will never live a life of abundance. If we start thinking about our money in terms of investing instead of spending, it will change the way we spend our money. Invest in things that will get you to where you want to be.

Invest in your physical self - It's true that when we look good, we feel good. Our physical appearance can be a source of dissatisfaction. It can affect our overall mood and the way that we view ourselves. Invest time and money in your physical health. Your physical health can keep you from achieving your desired goals.

Day 14

Invest in Yourself

Write down two ways you can invest in your personal happiness. Do you want to take a class, lose weight, or write a book? What steps do you need to take to make the investment?

Investment 1

_____
_____
_____

Steps

  1.
  2.

Investment 2

_____
_____
_____

Steps

1.

2.

Day 15

Stay Committed

Sometimes getting started isn't the issue. The bigger issue is staying committed and completing the project. Life happens and other responsibilities take us away from completing the project. It's easy to get sidetracked and abandon the project completely. Stay committed and finish what you start.

Day 15

Stay Committed

Identify at least two action steps you will take to ensure that you stay committed to reaching your goal.

Action Step 1:

_____
_____
_____
_____
_____
_____
_____

Action Step 2:

_____
_____
_____
_____
_____
_____
_____

Accountability

Day 16

Tracking My Daily Progress

What I did today.	What I could have done.

Plan for tomorrow:

_____
_____
_____
_____
_____
_____
_____
_____
_____
_____
_____
_____
_____
_____
_____

Day 17

Tracking My Daily Progress

What I did today.

What I could have done.

Plan for tomorrow:

_____
_____
_____
_____
_____
_____
_____
_____
_____
_____
_____
_____
_____
_____

Day 18

Tracking My Daily Progress

What I did today.	What I could have done.

Plan for tomorrow:

_____
_____
_____
_____
_____
_____
_____
_____
_____
_____
_____
_____
_____
_____

Day 19

Tracking My Daily Progress

What I did today.   What I could have done.

Plan for tomorrow:

_____
_____
_____
_____
_____
_____
_____
_____
_____
_____
_____
_____
_____
_____

Day 20

Tracking My Daily Progress

What I did today.

What I could have done.

Plan for tomorrow:

_____
_____
_____
_____
_____
_____
_____
_____
_____
_____
_____
_____
_____

Day 21

Tracking My Daily Progress

What I did today.

What I could have done.

Plan for tomorrow:

_____
_____
_____
_____
_____
_____
_____
_____
_____
_____
_____
_____
_____
_____

Day 22

Tracking My Daily Progress

What I did today.   What I could have done.

Plan for tomorrow:

_____
_____
_____
_____
_____
_____
_____
_____
_____
_____
_____
_____
_____
_____

Day 23

Tracking My Daily Progress

What I did today.	What I could have done.

Plan for tomorrow:

_____
_____
_____
_____
_____
_____
_____
_____
_____
_____
_____
_____
_____
_____

Day 24

Tracking My Daily Progress

What I did today.

What I could have done.

Plan for tomorrow:

_____
_____
_____
_____
_____
_____
_____
_____
_____
_____
_____
_____
_____
_____

Day 25

Tracking My Daily Progress

What I did today.	What I could have done.

Plan for tomorrow:

_____
_____
_____
_____
_____
_____
_____
_____
_____
_____
_____
_____

Day 26

Tracking My Daily Progress

What I did today.	What I could have done.

Plan for tomorrow:

_____
_____
_____
_____
_____
_____
_____
_____
_____
_____
_____
_____
_____
_____

Day 27

Tracking My Daily Progress

What I did today.   What I could have done.

Plan for tomorrow:

_____

_____

_____

_____

_____

_____

_____

_____

_____

_____

_____

_____

_____

_____

Day 28

Tracking My Daily Progress

What I did today.	What I could have done.

Plan for tomorrow:

_____

_____

_____

_____

_____

_____

_____

_____

_____

_____

_____

_____

_____

_____

Day 29

Tracking My Daily Progress

What I did today.   What I could have done.

| | |
| | |

Plan for tomorrow:

_____
_____
_____
_____
_____
_____
_____
_____
_____
_____
_____
_____
_____
_____

Day 30

Tracking My Daily Progress

What I did today.   What I could have done.

Plan for tomorrow:

_____
_____
_____
_____
_____
_____
_____
_____
_____
_____
_____
_____
_____
_____

CONGRATULATIONS!!!

You've completed...

IGNITE: A 30-Day Guide to Get You to Your Next Level and Achieving Your Goals

One major goal of this guide was to get you into the habit of strategically planning and achieving a goal.

I invite you to share your experience and thoughts. Visit my website at www.devoniareed.com/contact.

Here's to your greatness!

Devonia

www.ingramcontent.com/pod-product-compliance
Lightning Source LLC
Chambersburg PA
CBHW072210090426
42740CB00012B/2463